Praise for *Beautiful Chaos*

"The poems are so beautifully observed and shared. The words awaken the magic of life by celebrating the ordinary. They remind you of what once was, while beautifully planting you in the now. I just want to go back to the start and read them all again. A beautiful companion to keep by my side."

—GIOVANNA FLETCHER, AUTHOR OF *HAPPY MUM, HAPPY BABY*

"Jess's words weave their way straight to the core of the motherhood experience. Beautifully heartfelt, inspiringly poignant, and therapeutically validating."

—ANNA MATHUR, AUTHOR OF *RAISING A HAPPIER MOTHER*

"Feeling seen and understood in motherhood is rare in our judgmental, advice-laden world. Jess's beautiful words weave their way past your exhaustion, doubt, and guilt—straight to soothe your soul. Reading this book feels like a much-needed long exhale."

—ZOE BLASKEY, FOUNDER OF *MOTHERKIND*

"Jess guides you right into the heart of motherhood with her poignant and piercing style and is unafraid to take you into the tender places of life as a mother. *Beautiful Chaos* will remind you of the joyous moments, the moments that bring tears to your eyes, and the moments you find yourself on your knees. Above all, this new collection of Jess's beautiful poetry reassures you that you are not alone. Jess's words are healing, powerful, honest, and raw. She takes me right back to those tender newborn days, the mayhem of toddlerhood, and through life with a growing child, and in doing so reminds me of just how far I have come."

—TRACY GILLETT, FOUNDER OF *RAISED GOOD*

Beautiful Chaos

On Motherhood, Finding Yourself,
and Overwhelming Love

JESSICA URLICHS

G. P. PUTNAM'S SONS
NEW YORK

PUTNAM
— EST. 1838 —

G. P. PUTNAM'S SONS
Publishers Since 1838
an imprint of Penguin Random House LLC
1745 Broadway, New York, NY, 10019
penguinrandomhouse.com

Trade edition ISBN 9798217178018
Ebook ISBN 9798217178025

Printed in the United States of America
1st Printing

The authorized representative in the EU for product safety and compliance
is Penguin Random House Ireland, Morrison Chambers, 32 Nassau Street,
Dublin D02 YH68, Ireland, https://eu-contact.penguin.ie.

For the mothers who walk each other home

Beautiful Chaos

Contents

Introduction

I was five when I wrote my first poem, and I discovered then how exciting it could be to read and write about something simply ordinary. I have written my whole life, mostly for myself, but somewhere along the way poetry changed for me; it became a way to turn the mundane into magic instead. Only since becoming a mother have I been reminded that the ordinary is extraordinary – my children have reminded me of that, and of my five-year-old self.

But as sacred and tender as early motherhood was for me, it also came with its struggles, so I wrote about those too. The highs, the lows, the confusion, the loss of identity, the becoming, the brutal and beautiful ways our children hold mirrors up to us. I decided to share my poems online (after a lot of nudges from my husband). It was incredibly scary being so vulnerable and facing the world, and it was also like one long exhale.

What started as scribbles in the notepad app on my phone soon became poems and prose that were shared far and wide. They started to create a ripple effect of sorts: other mothers were saying 'same', and expressing their vulnerability. Before long I was surrounded by this beautiful online village (for me that is what it felt like), the same one that encouraged me to write a book. Sharing these honest words with you all is also cathartic and healing for me, because motherhood is messy, and beautiful, and hard and humbling. We adore our children and sometimes miss ourselves. It's so nuanced and, somehow, no matter the different paths we are on, we're connected through motherhood. So yes, it's scary when I think about my exposed heart on paper travelling the world, but then I think about who's reading my heart and I know it's OK, because 'they'll get it'.

I hope these pieces remind you of a time that was, or ground you in the time you're in now.

I hope you feel seen in all this beautiful chaos.

Welcome to Motherhood

When I entered motherhood
I walked through a little door
'This is Motherhood,' it read
Everyone sat there in stripey tops
Exchanging pleasantries
Things scattered all over the floor
Bags overflowing
Nervous smiles
Connected by motherhood
Disconnected by unspoken truths
Then someone said
'I love being a Mum, but this is also really hard,'
And suddenly I didn't feel alone any more.

Then someone
said 'I love being
a mum, but this
is also really hard,'
And suddenly
I didn't feel alone
any more.

BEAUTIFUL CHAOS, JESSICA URLICHS

Mother in Waiting

It's often said that I am made for this
Though sometimes I'm unsure
Because a mother wasn't waiting in
The girl I was before.

She didn't lie in restless slumbers
Memories made of night
And when the sky's outfit would change
She'd struggle to see the light.

She'd never been so still before
While her heart continued to travel
She'd never felt so put together
While the stitching of her unravelled.

She'd never known the waves of pain
That were woven into her bones
How to move without their weight
Or how to dance alone.

She'd never been this shape before
Her body sore and broken
Where life did grow, her heart a home
Its door forever open.

She'd never known a relationship
Could balance on mountain ridges
An ocean in between them
As they built their tiny bridges.

She'd never known how love could change
A person to a place
How home is found in the way we're held
In their smell, or in their face.

She'd never felt this kind of weight
Or how time could hold its breath
How silence could be deafening
How to give when there's nothing left.

She'd never had to pretend to know
Question countlessly if she was wrong
And learn one day she wasn't pretending
And she'd known all along.

Her feelings never leaked like rivers
Her time, never so poor
Yet richer in the ways
That didn't matter as much before.

She didn't know that nature could
Be placed upon her chest
How watching them grow was a type of calm
That meant she would never rest.

So though they say I was made for this
I'm not sure I agree
It wasn't I that made the mother
But motherhood that made me.

Carrying You

I carried you.
In a heartbeat you were one too.
The beat of mine,
The first song I sang to you.
Through pain and a force like no other, I carried you
into this world.
My skin and smell, your first intuition.
Breathing beside you, as you breathed life into me.
With tired bones and heavy eyes,
I carried you.
With my sore body and full heart,
I carried you.
With an aching love,
Our hearts whispering to each other as you fell asleep.
Though I will cry, and you will too.
We'll continue to sail along,
Led by you.
With this, I promise
to always carry you.
What a privilege to be loved like this.
The sleep will come.
The shore will come.
So I understand if you want to be here.
With one breath at a time.

I will carry you.
For as long as you need.
Because you carry me too.

What a privilege to be loved like this.

BEAUTIFUL CHAOS, JESSICA URLICHS

Before We become Two

Soon we won't be one.
We won't move to the same rhythm,
our heartbeats won't drum together from within.
This will be the last time I hold you this close.
One day you will be on your way,
and oh the treasures you will find,
the places you'll discover,
the things you will achieve.
It's impossible right now, in this moment,
to think I won't bear witness to it all.
How one day someone else will share your secrets and moods,
and know you much better than me.
You will tell stories I've never heard before,
while ours will echo through my heart for ever.

It was You

It wasn't long ago.
I saw you, and I fell.
Our very first encounter
I hold you, and I'm held.

Both between two worlds,
and you were coming home.
So new yet so familiar,
I know you, and I'm known.

Our hearts had met before,
an introduction in a dream.
The way you are my mirror,
I see you, and I'm seen.

I know you like a memory,
how skin to skin does yearn,
and when I'm feeling lost,
you're my steady, slow return.

Like a body knows to heal,
like the stars that burn above,
you mould to me like clay, and
I love you, and I'm loved.

It's like we've lived a thousand lives,
to each, we've both belonged.
It was you, my darling,
all this time.
It was you, all along.

It was you,
my darling,
all this time.
It was you,
all along.

BEAUTIFUL CHAOS, JESSICA URLICHS

Baby Blues

I sit on the hospital bed as a new mother,
which I became in mere seconds, to a perfectly healthy baby.
The river running down my face must mean I'm ungrateful.

'Mama, wipe away those tears.'

The congratulatory messages flood in:
'You must be overwhelmed with happiness,'
'Enjoy every minute.'
It's not their fault, I've said it too, it's what we say to new
mothers, isn't it?

'Mama, wipe away those tears.'

Look at what I have! I don't deserve to feel sad, let's throw that
emotion in the corner, with the postpartum underwear.
Nothing to see here.

'Mama, wipe away those tears.'

Why do I feel like a prisoner?
Why are these four walls closing in?
You have a roof over your head, you have a lovely home.
Some people live on the street!

'Mama, wipe away those tears.'

My body feels different, it looks different.
But many women would kill for your silvery stripes,
the lines of motherhood, look at what it gave you!

'Mama, wipe away those tears.'

I have a husband who is the definition of the word 'father'.
I know some women struggle without support.
See? You have it so good!

'Mama, wipe away those tears.'

I don't know this new me, I haven't met her before,
I'm doubting her a lot.
But you're alive, you're breathing, be thankful!

'Mama, wipe away those tears.'

I can't feel sad, there's no room for my sadness
with all that's going on.
My heart is full, but I'm running on empty
and I'm overwhelmed.
My body has broken and the pain is still in my bones.
My life has changed direction in an instant and I just need to feel
it all for a moment and cry without judgement, without question.
I stand here in the shower touching my spongy belly and I'm
alone in here for the first time in nine months, the sprays of
water drown away my tears.

I know you compare others' misfortunes against my
non-existent ones in the attempt to dam this river.
But my sadness belongs to me, it doesn't need to be measured.
I may not understand it either.
But please let me cry these tears
So I can feel lighter again.
So I can be the mother I am destined to be.
Without this shade of blue.
Because I am lucky,
I'm strong.
We are unbelievably strong.

All I See is You

Mama,

I can't see past you right now,
I'm so small and everything's a little blurry.

All I see is you.

When you feel alone, like the walls are closing in,
remember I'm here too. I know your world has changed
and the days feel a little lonely. But they aren't lonely for me.

You are my everything.

When you feel like you don't know what you're doing, you're
making it look easy to me. Even though we're still getting to
know each other, you know me better than anyone.

I trust you.

When you think some nights you'll never sleep again, you will.
We both will. But I'm scared right now. I promise I'm not
manipulating you. I just need your smell and comfort. Do you
feel that tug in your heart when we're apart? I do too.

I miss you.

When you feel as if you've achieved nothing,
please know, my cup has never been so full.
The days that get away from you will be some of my best
memories of us playing together on the ground.

I love you.

When you feel like you don't know who you are any more, when
you turn away from the mirror. That face will be the one I look
to when I achieve something, the one I search for in a
crowd. The reason for my first smile.

You're perfect to me.

When you feel like the weight of it all is heavy
in your heart, please know I've never felt lighter.
Can I lay here with you a little longer?
I won't always need you like this.

But I need you right now.

When you feel as if you have nothing left to give,
when I see your hands outstretched at me, pleading.
When we're both crying. I wish I could talk, but I can't.
If I could, I would tell you,

There's a reason I chose you.

I can't see past you right now, Mama, because you are my world.
It will get bigger, soon enough.

But for now,

All I see is you.

That face will be the one I look to when I achieve something, the one I search for in a crowd. The reason for my first smile.

BEAUTIFUL CHAOS, JESSICA URLICHS

Days of a Newborn
(and they really are just days)

The sunlight threatens to pour in, but the curtains are drawn at strange times. Beds unmade, hair tied up permanently, which becomes matted eventually.

Clothes on day three, you don't even put them away any more. There are pillows everywhere, things everywhere, like a tiny hoarder has come to stay. The TV is on at 2 a.m., reruns of a series while you learn about each other, how to feed, your limits, your love, you're likely to forget so many of these precious details.

Lost in the fog, found later when you realize they are a newborn no longer. Their clothes are bigger, nappies a size up, a few maybe; the little scrunch of them is fading.

You'll grieve for the tiny fingernails, the eyes that try to focus on you, the flailing arms, the little noises they make as they soften into you, their perfect little head that fits in the crook of your arm, how their scent is your skin's perfume.

This exhausting intimacy.

Yes, beautiful things can make you cry.

How you can grieve the passing-by even if you don't want another baby. And that last first smile, you'll marvel at how it changes and stays the same.

If only there was a way to visit every little version, a mosaic of mirrors at any one time. One you could look at and see all of them, and all the different yous would stare back too.

Dear Mama

I don't remember if our house was big or small,
or if we rented or owned.

I don't remember if you had a fancy car, or if we had to take the bus.

I don't remember if the house was clean and tidy,
or if it was covered in laundry and scattered toys.

I don't remember if my pram was new or second-hand,
or if I had the latest new toy or designer clothes.

I don't remember if you were dressed up,
or if your face was bare, it always looked perfect to me.

I don't remember if you had a lot of money,
or whether you lived pay cheque to pay cheque.

I don't remember if we went out every day,
or went on expensive holidays.

I don't remember how sometimes you got angry,
or cried or had to walk out of the room to take a breath.

I don't remember a schedule, a checklist,
or any expectations other than just you.

BEAUTIFUL CHAOS, JESSICA URLICHS

What I do remember is feeling safe.

I remember your comfort and how you kept me warm.

I remember your face above me when I cried for you.

I remember you would feed me when I was hungry
and comfort me when I was in pain.

I remember your smell and how it would send me off to sleep,
sometimes at 2 a.m., then again at 4 a.m.

I remember your smile; it was the first reason I smiled.

I remember how you played with me and got down on the
ground with me, before I could get up.

I remember you taught me about love before
anything else and how it was my constant.

I remember knowing it was the only thing I ever really needed,
and you gave that to me, I never had to work for it, I relaxed in it.

Thank you for teaching me that love has no limits, that it's
unconditional and honest.

This is what I will remember, Mama.

Thank you for giving me the best memories of all.

Thank you for teaching me that love has no limits, that it's unconditional and honest.

BEAUTIFUL CHAOS, JESSICA URLICHS

My World

For I was your sun,
the only warmth you needed before you saw
a sunrise with your own eyes.

I was your star,
before they dusted across your gaze
with possibility and wonder.

I was your moon,
your only pull, before you noticed the comforting
light in the night's blanket.

I was your universe for such a short while,
until you saw there was so much more.

But I will always be the earth,
your roots grew here.

And you will always be my world.

*I will always
be the earth,
your roots
grew here.*

*And you
will always
be my world.*

BEAUTIFUL CHAOS, JESSICA URLICHS

From One Mom to a Mother

People will paint you pictures about motherhood in rainbows;
you will forget that rain comes first.
The brightness of that rainbow will always outshine the grey,
but it's OK to talk about the grey, you should.

You will rise up in the dead of the night, time after time.
It will hurt; your bones will ache. You'll swear across
pillowcases as to whose turn it is to get up.
But you will sleep again.

You will question your identity; you will miss her.
But maybe no one told you the pieces of the puzzle
go back together from the inside out.
You will find yourself again.
There were two people born that day.

You will cry, your baby will cry.
Some evenings as a hush finally falls over your mess-ridden
house, the sound will be ringing in your ears.
But you will also laugh until you cry.
There is so much to look forward to.

You'll wonder if you're doing everything right,
you'll panic, second-guess, Google-search,
you'll wonder if you have enough for your baby.
Your baby has you; you are enough.

You'll be busy, yet also feel as if you're achieving nothing.
You're achieving everything that truly matters
in this precious moment.

That laundry? You'll be folding those tiny clothes away
into storage soon, sooner than you realize.
I'm not saying to enjoy every moment, you won't, but these
moments do pass.
Don't wish for it too much.

Some days will be a lucky dip with the mood in the house.
Don't try and do everything the same as the day
before so they have that long lunch nap.
You will have good days and bad days.
That's normal.

You will have days where you'll feel depleted from all the giving.
Try, really do try to fill your cup and not just everyone else's.
That doesn't make you selfish, it makes you a better mother.

You'll suddenly think of your own mother and
everyone who did this before you.
You'll have a new-found respect for each and every
mother or father climbing this same mountain.
You'll fall, but keep climbing.
The view is beautiful and so is the view behind you.

You might think some days you can't do this.

That it seems impossible.

But you can.

You are.

With each season comes change.

It isn't easy.

But it's so, so worth it.

There were two people born that day.

BEAUTIFUL CHAOS, JESSICA URLICHS

I Would Tell Her

If I could go back, I would tell her . . .

That one day she'll look back once the fog has cleared and realize those days were filled with magic. The type of magic you only see long after the trick. The beauty and then the bittersweet.

I'd tell her that the memories she'll lose herself in won't just be the milestones, but those long nights. She will never forget the pain of fatigue, but nostalgia will colour her memory and she'll find herself aching to breathe in those cuddles again.

I'd tell her about the tears, that with each cry she is learning. I'd tell her I'm not just talking about her baby.

I'd tell her she'll have alone time again, but it will feel like two hearts wandering in different directions. She'll ask if it will always feel that way. I'd tell her I don't know yet.

I'd tell her that her eyes will close, the sun will rise, but in between those moments she'll feel so alone in the company of the stars. I'd tell her each of those stars is another mother feeling exactly the same way, that she is never alone.

I'd tell her she doesn't need to be the perfect mother,
and the moment she believes there's such a thing
is the moment she believes she is failing.

I'd tell her that she is moving mountains,
even when she loses her footing.
Especially when she loses her footing.

I'd tell her in some ways it gets easier, but for every first
there is a last. The hardest part is not realizing till later that a
chapter has closed and you're turning back the pages trying to
pinpoint when you forgot to say goodbye to that
mispronounced word.

I'd tell her motherhood isn't a typical love story, motherhood is
the raw unedited version, with all the out-takes, which is what
makes it the most beautiful love story of all.

I would try to describe the power of the infinite love she will
feel, how it will consume her, scare her, comfort her.
That a love like this is a silent language that speaks volumes.

Only, I won't tell her these things, because she will forget,
like we all do, so that we can discover them
for ourselves, as we're meant to.

So instead I would simply tell her
that she is seen,
she is amazing,
and she is enough.

Motherhood isn't a typical love story, motherhood is the raw unedited version, with all the out-takes, which is what makes it the most beautiful love story of all.

BEAUTIFUL CHAOS, JESSICA URLICHS

My Season

My darling,
You were the storm that crashed against me
and took the shoreline with it.
The tide that rocked and soothed me.
The wind that had me mourning for the leaves you
kissed into autumn.
You were the fire that ignited mine when the darkness
took hold.
The sun showers that moved me in streams down my cheeks.
The warmth that breathed life into my core.
My roots grounded.
My heart soaring.
You were the seasons they spoke of.
Ever-changing and blooming.
For I thought I was growing you,
when you were growing me too.

*For I thought
I was growing you,
when you were
growing me too.*

BEAUTIFUL CHAOS, JESSICA URLICHS

Mother's Skin

We may not love the skin we're in postpartum.
But they do.
We may see the scars and stripes of repair.
But they don't.
We hang on to the looseness, cry over the leakage and break
ourselves over what we 'should be'.
But they know of no comparison,
only the you of yesterday and the you of today.

This magic skin grew them from within.
It encased the body that nourished them for all those months,
the heart that physically grew bigger to accommodate the
increased volume of blood.

It stretched with them and broke and healed.
It was the first skin they knew,
the one that smelt of contentment in their
first introduction to the scary outside world.

This skin will continue to be that comfort throughout life,
in so many ways.

It's OK to not love it completely and
miss the body we had before.
It's OK to not see ourselves through their eyes.

but if we want them to love the skin they're in,
we need to find peace in our own.

Embrace this new kind of beauty.
The real kind.
The one we need to talk about more.

*If we want them
to love the skin
they're in, we need
to find peace in
our own.*

BEAUTIFUL CHAOS, JESSICA URLICHS

I was Told

I was told my world would change.
I was told my house would change.
I was told I wouldn't sleep.
I was told I'd lose my sanity and myself.
I was told my body would change.
And so would my bank balance.
I was told my life would change.
But they forgot to tell me I would change.
And I did.
In the best way.
Because of you.

Maybe they were saving the best for last.

I Love You

I love you.
I hope you know that.
But I'm so small and I can't say it yet.
So the tears will come when I need you,
and sometimes I feel yours too.
I know you ache, but I ache for you.
Maybe we feel the same?
When it's dark around me and your face comes into view,
I know everything will be OK.
Do you know that too?
I just want to tell you,

I love you.
But I can't just yet.
So I'll stretch out my arms instead,
I'll protest and fuss when you put me down.
When all I want is your smell, my comfort, a wholeness.
Because you smell like the two of us, as if we were one.
You're all I know.
All I need.
I can't wait to know more about the you before me,
but right now it's 'us'.
One day I will tell you,

I love you.
When I gaze up at you, as soon as I find your eyes,
my whole world is in focus.
Maybe, we can both slow down together.
Orbit around each other, like we have nowhere else to be.
As if this will be no longer.
As if my smallness won't last.
I wish this moment could last for ever, and maybe one day
you will too.
These days are ours, as you whisper to me,

I love you.
When you kiss me goodnight.
As I fall asleep.
As we breathe each other in.
When I wake, again and again, searching for you.
While you're searching for you too.
While we find each other.
I know it is constant.
But you are my constant.
Because these days filled with nothing are everything to me.

And soon my head won't rest on your chest,
soon my cries will become words instead.
By watching you, my lips start to move,
the only feeling I've ever known, in a voice that feels new.
I'll smile up at you and say the words,

'I love you too.'

Dear Little One

When I look at you,

I see him.
When the sun splashes across the walls of your room in the
morning and pulls the hazel from your eyes.

I see me.
When you look at me from the side, that cheeky grin framed
with ringlets, a faded photograph brought to life.

I see him.
Those lips of yours, they're not mine, and when you smile
I melt because I'm taken to a place that's entirely new and
familiar all at once. The only way I could describe love.

I see me.
When you perform and put on your fairy wings,
and leap across the room. You are making sure I'm watching you,
and I catch myself wondering when that sparkle fades.
Thank you for bringing back mine.

I see him.
Your calm nature and the way you observe.
I'm quick to say your stubborn ways are him too,
but I know it's probably me. In fact, I love your strong will.

I see me.
The way you throw back your head and laugh,
the shape of your nose, the shape of your chin,
but the shape of your future, that will always be yours.

Because you're not me.
Or him.
You're you.

The reason I see us when I look at you
is because you are my hopes and dreams.
You are the love that gets me through.
You are the reflection in my eyes.

Dear little one,
there will be glimpses of us in you.
But it's you I will forever see,
when I look at me.

*There will
be glimpses
of us in you.
But it's you
I will forever see,
when I look at me.*

BEAUTIFUL CHAOS, JESSICA URLICHS

I'm Awake with You

Who's awake right now?
At night I sometimes wonder
Is every twinkling star outside
Another tired mother?
All in it together
But doing it alone
Soothing little cries
In the darkness of our homes
Is she stumbling down the hallway?
She's lost count how many times
Is she reaching across her bed
With the heaviest of eyes?
Perhaps mothers are connected
By the push and pull of string
The midnight hour dancing
And the tired songs we sing
Sat in chairs, hunched over cots
Or waiting at the door
Feeding, shushing, loving
While the world sleeps on some more
I know it can be lonely
I feel it sometimes too
Just so you know, in case it helps
I'm awake with you.

Is every twinkling star outside Another tired mother?

BEAUTIFUL CHAOS, JESSICA URLICHS

Magic

Magic can be familiar
and magic can be new,
it can be in knowing nothing else
than the love I have for you.
Magic is in your voice, your scent,
the beating of your heart.
Magic is how it whispered to mine
when everything was dark.
Magic isn't make-believe,
It's not in the unknown.
Magic is meeting someone new
who has always been your home.

Remembering You

Truth be told, if I was old
and we didn't know each other,
would the things that lived
inside me once
stay with me for ever?

Would I see your eyes in someone else,
would I feel it in my soul?
An intersection
of two stars aligned,
would I know it in my bones?

I never truly felt your weight
and though we never met,
will I carry your heart
and know your face?
Will I somehow not forget?

Will the universe between
my hand and womb
unfold within my dreams?
Will your smile, your cry,
your shadow feet
move through me like streams?

And though I never
knew your laugh,
I hear it all the time.
For maybe one day
our paths will cross,

and I'll remember,
when you were mine.

Postpartum is For Ever

Don't forget to call
when the due date's been and gone,
when all the excitement settles down,
and the days and nights are long.

Don't forget to message,
she needs to know you're there.
When all the hype around the news
begins to disappear.

Don't forget about her,
she may have one or two.
Even on a familiar path
the dynamic is still new.

And don't forget to invite her,
though she probably won't go.
To know you're thinking of her
means more than you could know.

So don't forget the mother,
she needs you more than ever.
Her baby may be older,
but postpartum is *for ever.*

Postpartum is for ever.

BEAUTIFUL CHAOS, JESSICA URLICHS

I'll Come to You When You Call

I sleep on the surface now
And I'll come to you when you call
My tired eyes adjust to the dark
You're a baby, after all.

And even when you're not
I'll come to you when you cry
When you're standing, calling from your cot
There will be no question why.

And when you're in a bigger bed
And calling down the hall
If monsters find you in your dreams
I'll come to you when you call.

And when you're staying at your friends
If you suddenly feel alone
I'll come to you when you call
And I'll bring us both back home.

And if the night should take a turn
No matter what you've done
I'm here, I'm here, I'm always here
I'll always be your mum.

There are no limits, or confines
No schedules and no rules
If you need me, I'll be there
I'll come to you when you call.

And if harder days should find you
With a family of your own
I'll come to you when you call
Please just pick up the phone.

But for now, I'll hold you in the night
You're still so very small
I hope you know I'll always show
Because I come to you when you call.

If you need me,
I'll be there
I'll come to you
when you call.

BEAUTIFUL CHAOS, JESSICA URLICHS

That First Smile

They didn't tell me
About that first time
How after that moment
Our worlds would align

They spoke of the birth
The moment we'd meet
Breathing you in
Being brought to my knees

Hovering in your doorway
Staring into your eyes
Willing you to tell me
What you only could in cries

I was fearful of those mornings
As everyone would leave
The room became smaller
It was harder to breathe

Pinching myself
because I had a new meaning
Pinching myself
Through the tears of feeding

Burp cloths and pumps
And nappy decor
Sprawled out with the pieces of
Me on the floor

Just like magic
This gift I was handed
The timing was perfect
Like nature had planned it

They told me it would come
That it may take a while
But never how I'd feel
When I saw that first smile

Motherhood in an instant
Became mine for the taking
Suddenly every last moment
Was history in the making

I was your reason
And you were mine
The moment our worlds
Stood still in time.

*I was your
reason
And you
were mine
The moment
our worlds
Stood still
in time.*

BEAUTIFUL CHAOS, JESSICA URLICHS

Hello, Old Friend

Today I saw an old friend from my past
She barely stopped, she was moving so fast.

Hurrying and shushing
And looking quite flushed
The frazzled kind
Not contoured with blush.

I had to double-take
Her brows in a frown
Her clothes mismatched
Her hair in a crown.

She carried herself differently
Tired and raw
But a beauty that shined
More visibly than before.

It wasn't the kind that we're used to seeing.
It's the kind that radiates from your very being.

She swayed side to side
A baby on her hip
As she stared in the distance
Chewing her lip.

I decided to approach and reconnect with this girl
To remind her that she was conquering the world.

She told me her life had completely changed
That the pieces of her had been rearranged
Pieces left for months on the floor
So it took her a while to feel whole once more.

Then she said, 'I get it now'
'This is who I'm meant to be'
And I actually believed her
As she stared back at me.

She was tired yet knowing
A world of content
In a place so new
For where she was meant.

I took a deep breath
As I left our embrace
From the girl in the mirror
With a smile on my face.

My Everything

I want to tell you everything I know,
carry you and guide you.
Yet somehow,
as your tiny finger points to things in wonder
and your eyes meet mine,
the paradigm shifts.
I once thought I was to show you the world,
when all along you came to show me.

*I once thought
I was to show
you the world,
when all along
you came to
show me.*

BEAUTIFUL CHAOS, JESSICA URLICHS

Thank You

Thank you for standing by me
Watching what I've gone through.
I forget sometimes through teary eyes
That you've had to go through it too.

The labour and the birth
While that pain was mine
Your hand was never far away
Your eyes never so wide.

My fear of being a new mother.
The onset of baby blues.
All the while you stayed strong for me
While you were quietly fearful too.

The early days of breastfeeding.
The trials and the tears.
You were always helping with the latch
While I was screaming in your ear.

See sometimes I forget
As hard as it was on me
You had to watch me in this pain
As you sat there helplessly.

Trying to remember things from antenatal
Taking turns getting up in the night
Feeling the fog of the fourth trimester
In your own given right.

The daily battles I have at home
Which you feel as you walk in the door
But always with a smile and open arms
Taking the weight off me once more.

You've seen me raw and at my limit.
You've seen me vulnerable and small.
All the while you've remained my rock
And loved me through it all.

You don't sit on the sidelines
Instead you sit by my side
While we learn this all together
On this beautiful but bumpy ride.

Even though you say sometimes
You don't know what you can do.
You've done it without even knowing
For being their father and just being you.

18 Summers

People say we only have 18 summers, like I'm counting
down to the longest winter.
Like the sun won't always set in your eyes,
bringing summer to me for ever.

People say, 'Blink and you'll miss it.' But it's when I blink that the
images of yesterday dance across my mind. Sometimes I close
my eyes a little longer to remember, I didn't miss a thing.

People say you lose yourself in motherhood, but you had me all
along. You took a lot out of me but gave me so much more.
You were the only search party I needed.

People talk of how the seasons pass.
But I take them with me, each one no matter how beautiful,
no matter how hard, is part of our growth.

People say, 'Enjoy every minute,' and sometimes I don't.
But I enjoy you.
I enjoy being your mum.
You could have been anyone, I'm so thankful you're you.

People talk of 'back in my day', of 'We did this, and you turned out OK.' There's so much old advice, there's so much new. They lay it on thick like concrete over roots.

People talk of sleep, but we don't measure your worth by the hours your eyes are closed. And while we've been cracked open, it was to bring you in, to hold you a little longer.

And they talk of 18 summers.
As if the first ripple of your life won't always be the waves in mine. Bringing summer to me, for ever.

You could have been anyone, I'm so thankful you're you.

BEAUTIFUL CHAOS, JESSICA URLICHS

Just You Wait and See

'Just you wait and see.'

You'll hear those words a bit, Mama,
in fact you probably already have.

You'll be reminded that if you think you're tired now,
'Just you wait and see.'

If you think you're sore now,
'Just you wait and see.'

If you think you're busy now,
'Just you wait and see.'

There's so much you'll be told, and a lot of it is true,
but there's so much they don't say too.

They'll tell you the birth is painful, but did they tell you about
your strength? The strength you always had that could bring a
life into this world and shortly after leave you breathless?

They'll tell you it's the most rewarding job in the world,
but did they tell you they felt lonely some days?

That some days a rain cloud followed them around and they
mourned for more than dishes, washing and burp cloths. You'll
wonder how this can be so hard when loving them comes so easy.

They'll tell you that you'll lose yourself in motherhood,
but did they tell you to stop looking for her? It's still you,
just a new version, reborn as a mother.
She is coming to find you, so stand still for a moment.

They'll tell you of how fast they grow, and it's true.
One minute you're their whole world, the next they're
venturing down the hallway and room by room
it becomes bigger. It's sad when they leave versions of
themselves behind, but be proud, Mama, they're going places!

They'll tell you they hope you have a good baby, one who sleeps
through the night, maybe you'll be lucky? But did they tell you to
just surrender? The pain of fatigue is haunting, but they need
you right now. It's not because you didn't follow some schedule,
it's because you're their home, they are all good babies.

They'll tell you about the worry and the guilt, how some days it'll
consume you. But did they tell you Mum guilt seeks out the
good mums? The ones who have so much love they are winded
by it? Mum guilt will lie to you, so remember, you are enough,
you are more than enough.

They'll tell you about that first smile, about how
precious that moment would be. But did they tell you it
happens when you need it the most? The fourth trimester
can be tough, but almost as if planned that smile will save you.

They'll tell you it's a strain on your relationship,
and it can be, it's not easy. But did they tell you that it won't
always be this way? One day you'll have your nights back again,
the house will be clean, and the rooms will be silent and your
heart will be in pieces because of it.

It's a journey together where the best isn't just yet to come.
The best is yesterday, today and tomorrow.
That's motherhood.
And it's magic.

Just you wait and see.

They are all good babies.

BEAUTIFUL CHAOS, JESSICA URLICHS

Mama, You're Beautiful

I see you, Mama, and something about you has changed.

I don't think I've ever seen you more beautiful.
You may have forgotten this among the throes of
motherhood, and find it hard to see it through the blur
of these early days, but I see you.

Your hair may not be blow-waved like it used to be, but now it's
a crown above your head, messy and perfectly imperfect.

Your hands seem different, they may not be as manicured, but
they're warm and comforting. They're stronger, as they hold the
world, and the touch of those fingertips are someone's world.

Yes, your heart aches, but it's never stretched and been so
swollen before with love, so of course it will ache sometimes.

You've always carried yourself well, but now you seem more
womanly, stronger, yet quietly vulnerable.

Your eyes are begging to see some darkness for more than a
couple of hours at a time. I know you're tired, but they still
shine, especially when you look at your miracle.

Your body may feel different, but under those baggy clothes is the greatest gift to you and to what you've created. It nurtures, it bends and breaks, it's resilient, it's exceptional.

You may be feeling lonely at times, or tired of being at home, but you truly look beautiful here, like all of a sudden home has a new meaning. You are someone's home.

Your smile has changed, it's now one that knows things, secrets of contentment. There's not as much energy behind it right now, but it's never been so pure.

The way you sit there, holding your baby like it's an extension of yourself, a natural, I've never seen anything so perfect.

I'm so proud of you and how amazing you are.

Mama, you're beautiful.

Home has a new meaning. You are someone's home.

BEAUTIFUL CHAOS, JESSICA URLICHS

The Paradox of Motherhood

You can mourn the girl you were
and love who you are now,
you can build a beautiful life around
the days that come crashing down.

You can feel the sunlight on your face
from the bottom of the ocean,
you can watch your world as it stands still,
and never more in motion.

You can know where you are going
when your alignment's slowly shifting,
you can gasp under the waves,
or they can hold you while you're drifting.

You can trace their face for hours
until they fall asleep,
you can whisper that you'll remember it all,
a promise you may not keep.

You can be their universe
move mountains with a touch,
you can feel scared for no other reason
than you love them, so very much.

You can wish away the loneliness
when the nights are coffee black,
you can study the landscape of their skin
and look forward, while looking back.

You can feel closer to your partner
though the ground beneath you is shaking,
you can never be more tired
while something within you is waking.

You can exhale the hardest days
while you're still holding your breath,
you can give yourself over and over
when it feels like there's nothing left.

You can learn the art of holding on
while also letting go,
you can have no idea what you are doing,
even though deep down you know.

You can think back to before you loved them,
a time ago that felt so long,
you can hold that tiny hand in yours,
and never feel so strong.

You can take with you the old
while weaving in the new,
you can pick your tired bones up,
asking, why nobody told you.

You can watch them like you've known them
forever and a day,
you can rest assured you have,
as it was meant to be this way.

You can be entangled,
beginning, middle, end,
you can wonder where your place is
knowing simply, it is them.

It's only confusing when you think
it's one without the other,
because opposites can grow in gardens,
Within you as a mother.

It makes no sense and complete sense
and turns you inside out,
and love can hold you – *and it will,*
through all the tears and doubt.

Because motherhood is fast and slow
it broke and made me whole,
a divide that only multiplies
within your heart and soul.

When I Say You are Everything

When I say you are everything,
I mean you are every finger that wraps itself around one
of mine. I mean you are every breath I take, even when it
bites on those frosty mornings. I mean you are every
letter, every lyric, every beautiful sentence in a love note,
and still, there are no words. I mean you are every dream
and every tear, every smile, every wake.
You are every beat of my heart, even the ones before we
met, the slow and steady rhythm

to

get

to

you.

I mean you are every inch that I've stretched and carried,
such little maps of us. Every cloud's silver lining, every
rainbow, every view where the sun strips back the sky,
where the birds sing who survived the night, where I'm
standing on a mountain and the future comes to greet
me, and on a clear day you can see everything.

Hand-me-downs

I'm so thankful to the mamas who gave me hand-me-downs.
They're not just clothes,
or hand-me-downs.
They're little pick-me-ups to another mother.
Gathered-together moments of the shortest and longest time.
They're past memories and the promise of new ones.
They're tiny treasures pulled out of storage,
outgrown stages, well-worn stories.
They're faded knees and a full heart.
They're so much more than hand-me-downs.
And you only know that when you become a mother.

You'll Always be My Baby

You'll always be my baby
just heavier to hold

You'll always be my beginning
but a comfort that feels old

You'll always be my heartbeat
a familiar but new sound

You'll always be the ticking clock
in a world you made slow down

You'll always be my worry
when you trip and when you fall

You'll always be my tears
the happiest of them all

You'll always be my constant
the pulse of our home

You'll always be my calling
more so when I'm alone

You'll always be my journey
I'm taken away with you

You'll always be my weakness
and a strength I never knew

You'll always be my final thoughts
even on those harder days

You'll always be my for ever
and forever be my always

You'll always be my reason
even when I'm grey and old

You'll always be my baby
just heavier to hold.

*You'll always
be my baby
just heavier
to hold.*

BEAUTIFUL CHAOS, JESSICA URLICHS

Things I Would Tell Myself
as a New Mother

Breastfeeding might be one of the hardest things
you will ever do. It may also turn into one
of the most beautiful things too. But if it doesn't work out,
remember this is such a short
part of the journey of raising this little human.
Do what is right for you both,
your mental health matters.

You aren't the only one who has cried in the shower,
while feeding, with your hands
through the cot bars at 2 a.m. It's a privilege
being someone's everything, and it's also
incredibly hard. I promise you will sleep again.

You might bond with your baby instantly,
you might not. Maybe you had a traumatic birth,
maybe it was empowering. Regardless,
that bond will come. We have all experienced tough
times in our lives, but never this love;
this kind of love is so big it hurts.

You will learn a lot about yourself, about your instincts,
about regulating your emotions,

about apologizing, about who you want to be,
for them, but also for you. You'll learn a lot
about relationships, you'll become closer
with your partner in ways that may feel
distant at first. Be patient with it all.

Friendships may change; some will fade,
some will become stronger.
You've just had a baby, be gentle with yourself,
inhale, exhale, heal, and be.
You might feel like you've gone missing for a while,
but your true friends will never leave.

There will be parts about your old life you will miss,
that might confuse you.
But it's normal. You might put all of you into motherhood,
but motherhood is not all of
you. Turn your music on in the kitchen and dance,
create, laugh, do what you love when you
have time to catch your breath again.
Let them see that.

Please don't compare yourself to those you see online.
Your village might look different to
theirs, they may have a cleaner, they may have
children with different temperaments to
yours, they also just may not show the messy.
I promise you, we're all a little messy.

Get in the photo, please. You look perfect. Just get in the photo, you won't regret it.

Oh, and you're doing amazing.
Just in case no one told you that today.

Today You Turn One

It's been a year
Of watching you grow
Loving who you are now
Loving you of tomorrow.

It's been a year
Making friends with the moon
But I'd relive each night
Because I got to hold you.

It's been a year
Watching crawling become walking
Uncertainty become confidence
And soon you'll be talking.

It's been a year
Of us together
A newborn no longer
But my baby for ever.

It's been a year
Of you on my chest
You'll never remember it
But it's been one of my best.

It's been a year
Of first teeth and first smiles
Can we slow down a little?
Can we just stay a while?

It's been a year
Of two brand-news
The day I met me
Was the day I met you.

It's been a year
Our first trip round the sun
Happy birthday to you
Today you turn one.

You before Me

I wonder who you were, Mum,
the you, before I was me.
Before the branches of you shook,
and gave me all the leaves.

Did the giving leave you breathless?
And then did you give some more?
Was there any left for you
in that cup to pour?

And when you gave me life
did you live for yourself too?
Did you feel like a different person
when you entered a room?

And did you sacrifice a lot
all so you could have me?
I know you, but I wonder,
who you used to be.

Was I your making, and your mirror?
Did you hold me sometimes and cry?
Did the lion within you get stronger?
Or did it run away to die?

Mum, I know your life began,
before I came along,
but did the rhythm of my breath
give your life a sweeter song?

And that flame that lives inside you,
did it flicker, or did it grow?
The lighthouse that guided me all these years,
that now lives in my bones.

I wonder these things now, Mum,
as I hold my babies close.
The way that I now matter to them,
is what matters to me the most.

Did you feel completely grounded?
But with a smile that had changed?
Did it shape all that you do, and more?
Did you too feel rearranged?

And though you were my person,
were you still your person too?
Was it like unstitching parts of us,
to get back some of you?

And lastly, Mum, as I sway here,
I think I understand
just what it takes to be the moon,
the stars, and someone's land.

But sometimes I wish, in a parallel world
I could visit for just one day,
where you didn't know me, or who I was,
and you didn't know my name.

And I'd talk with you about all sorts,
your laughter like the sun,
and I'd recognize that smile
but with plans, so free and young.

And know you, just as I am now,
before your name was Mum.

I Grew a Baby while I Had a Baby

I grew a baby while I had a baby,
The voices became louder as my belly began to rise.
'This will be hard.'
'This will be hard.'
'This will be hard.'
I had become ripe for comments by faces I would soon forget.
People would talk of my hands being full, the divide
(that I would pull myself together though).
In the evening song I would soothe limbs inside and out,
humming and swaying through the doubt.
I met my baby when I had a baby, and I cried and loved and
wondered if 'they' were right.
But looking at them, looking at each other, was finding myself,
even all these years later.
The love
The love
The love.
It can be hard and just as you want it.
The things they don't say.
About having a baby when you have a baby.

The Wild Child

You might have the 'wild child'
The one who speaks their mind
The one who doesn't listen
Where patience is hard to find

The one who does it on their own
Who doesn't need your help
With stubborn ways, and on those days
Will turn you inside out

The one that they call 'naughty'
Where strangers roll their eyes
The one labelled as 'hard'
Who often yells, or cries

But often it's forgotten
These ones aren't really 'wild'
They're tiny humans learning
And, in fact, they're just a child

They're the ones who feel things deeply
Who will have a voice that's strong
They'll lead with that big heart of theirs
And stand up to what is wrong

They'll challenge our way of thinking
They're gentle, brave and bold
And they picked us to guide them
In a world that can feel cold

So maybe they seem 'hard' right now
But they'll change the way we live
With so much good to come, you'll see
With so, so much to give.

Blink and You'll Miss It

'Blink and you'll miss it,' they say.
But I didn't miss it, I was there.

I was there, placing you down to sleep on your back, elbows in
line with your shoulders, hands at your ears.
I always wondered why tiny babies slept that way.
Then you rolled over, then you were sitting, and now you're
jumping from the coffee table to the couch.

I was there, through the tears of breastfeeding, pinching my leg
or curling my toes. I wondered if I could do this again. Then one
day we were in the kitchen, I was stirring dinner and you were
feeding in my other arm, and I smiled, how did we get here?

I was there, pacing the hallway, squinting my eyes shut,
wishing the moment away. Shattered beyond measure at the
thought of another day on no sleep. I was there as you cuddled
into me, as we surrendered to each other. I still envelop you
into my arms, but you don't fold into me the same and
you tell me when you're ready for your cot now.

I was there, as they placed you on my chest, never more alive,
never more terrified. My world in my arms as I listened
to those tiny squawks. Now you're saying things like,
'I don't want to,' 'I love you' or 'Go 'way, Mummy.'

I don't remember when the nights got easier, but they did,
or when you stopped saying 'uggle' instead of 'cuddle',
or the moment I kissed those little feet and was
greeted with sweat instead of your signature newborn scent.

Oh, how I know I will miss this when I look
back through the rear-view mirror.
How I know that no matter how testing, memory
lane will be tree-lined with nostalgia.
Will I truly remember it as it was?
Or will I be trying to pin down a bubble?

When do all the becomings become goings or gones?

'Blink and you'll miss it,' they say.

But we don't miss it.
We miss saying goodbye to it.

A Letter to My Firstborn

My firstborn,

It was you who made me a mother.

It was you who stopped me in my tracks and
paved new ones for me.

It was you who reduced me to the rubble of myself,
and then built me back up stronger.

It was you who gave me so many reasons, but also reasons for
criticizing my body, for loving what it gave me,
for being comfortable in my own skin.

It was you who first turned the nights into weeks
and the years into days.

It was you who filled me with a type of gratitude
I'd never known, each breath you took filled my lungs,
each step you took was our journey together.

It was you who introduced me to so many firsts,
to a different type of love, heartache, and to me.

It was you who gave me a kind of confidence I never knew
I had within, a whisper turned roar, an exercised patience,
a worry that will live in my heart for ever.

It was you who unearthed me, things tucked away,
no longer buried, it was you who cracked me open.

It was you who showed me a different view of the world,
decisions, memories, dreams, are all shaped with you.

It was you I held as I cried in the early months, deep in the
trenches, lonely but in the best company.

Tired but never more alive.
It was you who got me through.

You're much older now.

But I'll always remember us in the quiet of the weekdays,
where we did nothing and everything.
Our chapter.
How it was you who made me a mother.

It was you who introduced me to so many firsts, to a different type of love, heartache, and to me.

BEAUTIFUL CHAOS, JESSICA URLICHS

I'm Your Safe Place

I get it, I get all of it.

The screams, the tears, the tantrums.

Your bottom lip drops and your eyes brim with emotions.
Sometimes you even turn away from me.
That one rips my heart in two.

Then the sun will peek through, and the smiles will come for
Daddy, and I'll be left here in the storm puddles.

I feel your pain because I'm also tired and torn, but I get it now.
I'm that place for you.

When you have a scary dream and you call 'Mummy',
because my hugs and the sound of my voice breathes
confidence into you.

The one that always has its lights on with
the open sign hanging in the window.

Yes, you can air your laundry here and forget to
wipe your feet on the doormat.

I'm that place where you can scatter your feelings
over the floor, and I won't sweep them under the rug.

I know at times you try to hold it all together.
You can unravel here.
And I won't judge you, I'll open my arms to you.
Please fall into them when you're ready.

You've come from a place where your only
expectation was to just be.
Suspended in warmth and safety.
Your beautiful rhythmic heartbeat mixing in with my own.

Out here it's different, not everyone will look at you how I do.
Expectations will be thrown at you unfairly
and at such a young age.
Not everyone will encourage you to take your time,
and that makes my heart ache.
But I promise you this: I will.

When you lock eyes on me in the crowd of chaos,
you see familiarity, security, love.

I am your safe place for you to feel.

The one whose shoulder fits your head just right.

Love is unconditional here;
the key will always fit and I don't keep receipts.

You're not at your worst, you're at your limit.
And my love for you is limitless.

I am your home.

Always know, you're safe here with me.

You're not at your worst, you're at your limit.
And my love for you is limitless.

BEAUTIFUL CHAOS, JESSICA URLICHS

The Every Mum

The gentle mum, the yelly mum
The 'can I just be both?' mum

The 'tomorrow will be better' mum
The 'just get through today' mum

A bit of a helicopter, 'here, let me'
The risk-taker, the adventurer
The 'just wait and see'
The 'don't make me laugh, or I might pee'

The 'penny for your thoughts' mum
The confident, outspoken mum
You think you know her story mum
You don't, so just be kind mum

The dressing gown, the coffee in hand
The yoga pants, some self-care planned
Watch *One Born Every Minute* mum
The 'ignorance is bliss' mum

I'm one and done, or what's two or five?
The only organic, or just eat to survive
The 'I need a moment alone' mum
The cannot be without them mum

Crunchy, yummy, whatever mum
Postpartum undies, saggy bum
Two years later cos they're comfy mum

The frazzled mum, the sweary mum
'I said truck, don't repeat that at Kindy' mum
The 'I can rap this whole song in the car' mum
I got 99 problems . . . and baby shark is one

The larger-body *real* mum
The skinny-body *real* mum
The 'just stop talking about my body' mum
Don't look at it, but what it's done!

The textbook mum, the earthy mum
the 'I have no idea what I'm doing' mum
The 'excuse the mess' (but it's tidy) mum
The anxious, hovering, worried mum

The work-out kind, the pay no mind
The mum tum, mum bun
5 p.m. wine

The stay-at-home, the working mum
The 'both are hard on my heart' mum
The crafty mum, 'let's whip up a cake'
The 'I'd rather poke out my eyes than bake'

But the thing is this,
you are good-enough mum
If it's dark and restful, not a peep
Or if you're cuddling them, whispering, 'Go the f*** to sleep'

Because when the day is over and done
I'm a little bit of every mum.

One to Two

You were all I knew,
before one became two.
You weren't my tiny baby any more,
even though a baby you were.
Just us, no longer.
No longer just us.
And when you both cried, I would cry too.
My first home.
My first teacher.

The bigger you felt in my arms,
the heavier my heart.
People would come over,
'Have some time with the baby,' they would say,
and they would take my baby away.
I felt I needed to pull over and ask for directions; the
neighbourhood was familiar but the street names had changed
and I wanted to find my way back to you.

Then you took her tiny hand in yours and
I realized what I had given you.
What I had given us.
Nothing felt harder,
but nothing was easier than loving you both.

There were days I couldn't divide myself,
where I'd fantasize of splitting myself in two,
but please know,
you walk around with my heart, as does she.
So in some ways I'll always be
in two places at once.

People would come over, 'Have some time with the baby,' they would say, and they would take my baby away.

BEAUTIFUL CHAOS, JESSICA URLICHS

Dear Friend

Dear Friend,

It's still me,

Well, sort of.

I'm here, but another version entirely.

I'm in a bubble of longing and love.

I know you messaged me this morning, or was it yesterday?
It's all a bit of a blur and my phone's buried somewhere on
my bedside table that has never felt so small.

I so badly want to reconnect with you but
I'm trying to reconnect with me too.

I'm cancelling a lot, and it's hard to say why; the anxiety
has held me prisoner here a bit and I want to talk about nothing,
and everything. I want to pour a wine and laugh with you.
But I don't know how to be the girl of yesterday.

I also want to try and get some sleep, but even when
I'm able to I'm scrolling through photos or
checking if he's breathing in his cot.

I've never had such fulfilment, but I feel a bit empty right now,
even though the room is full, even though my heart is too.

I'm still accepting that my milestones now are first smiles, the
way he now looks at me in true focus; I told my husband our
son must definitely know I'm his mother by now.
I wonder if there will be anything else I can talk about.
I think some days I'm still truly waiting for all this to hit me.

I'm a mother now.

My nights aren't popping bottles; they're pouring milk into
them or figuring out the latch. I'm trying to find time to eat a
full meal, or shower. Can you believe I plan that stuff now?
I'm not waking up with a hangover and texting you straight
away about last night's antics. I still feel hung over,
but I'm not the one who's been drinking all night.

My bones ache, my heart aches, and I also have a headache,
I think from this constant mum bun my hair lives in.

I'm not sure I can hold it all together. I know I don't
have to with you, but right now I just need to try.

This is my life right now, nap schedules, dressing gowns at
2 p.m., Google searches, doctor's appointments and
a constant reminder that my phone storage is full.
It's hard to swallow but I want to inhale it all.

Oh, it's a whirlwind, Friend, but one I'm glad to be caught up in.
Please keep checking in.
Please keep inviting me.
It means more than you know.

I'll be back.
In some shape or form.

Some Things I Know

Try to listen as if you have nothing to say after.
Water tends to solve restlessness, drinking it, splashing in it.
Stop worrying about their white clothes getting dirty.
Stop buying them white clothes.
You will not ruin them by sometimes saying the wrong thing.
Always buy more bananas than you think.
Hide spinach in smoothies, add berries for flavour.

Surrender to the sleep thing; it's less exhausting
than fighting it. You will sleep again, sort of.
If they won't eat their dinner then feed them the same
thing off your plate, or in their room, or in the bath.
They will have a favourite book; it won't be yours,
but you will read it 100 times anyway.

You won't need an alarm clock any more.
You won't be a gentle parent all of the time,
although you're trying.
If they're playing and laughing together it's usually
followed by crying.
Get a laundry hamper for every room; it's just easier.
Mum guilt gets the good mums.

Buy two of their favourite cuddly; if you know, you know.
You can try to hide in the pantry to devour that chocolate,
but they will sniff you out.
You don't need lots of fancy toys; they will enjoy
the box it came in, the TV remote, the dog bowls.
Saying 'it's spicy' only works for so long.
'I'll race you to bed' only works for so long.
Let them cling to you in bed; it won't be for ever.

Be willing to unlearn, so they can teach you.
Live in the moment when you remember to.
Don't believe everything you see online.
Toddlers can be savage; it's not just yours.
You don't need everything in that nappy bag, but on the
day you don't bring it, you'll need it.
Hours can pass by in five minutes, but as they say,
the years are short.

Get comfortable with public tantrums
and big emotions, yours too.
Talk about how craft is for daycare.
Attempt said craft at home, cry.
Mess can be cleaned, but it's OK if you're triggered by it.
Remember you are not just nurturing them but this life of yours
together. Do things for you too.

Apologize to them when you need to.
Don't apologize for them acting their age.
Buy two sizes up; hand-me-downs are even better.
Keep reinforcing you said 'truck', even though that won't work.

Take a deep breath; teach them about deep breathing.
Most of us don't know what we're doing,
but we will always show up.

Hold your arms out to them, even when you don't feel like it.
You probably need that hug more than they do.

Be willing to unlearn, so they can teach you.

BEAUTIFUL CHAOS, JESSICA URLICHS

Today You Turn Two

Not long ago
You brought with you the sun
You changed my world
I became a mum.

I've known love,
That much is true
But not like this
Not like you.

I'll celebrate your milestones
And with this I will try
To stay present through knowing
There are so many last times.

Your little clothes
Get packed away
Baby words more polished
With each new day.

You'll never be this small
So I'll treasure this time
One day when we cuddle
Your head will rest on mine.

All those nights
I sigh by your bed
Patting your back
Stroking your head.

One day I'll miss this
As I peek through your door
You'll drift off without me
My safe touch not needed any more.

Those bright eyes of yours
That mobilize your soul
Will change through the years
Carrying weights as you grow.

But when I look into them
I'll always see
That little baby
Who loves their mummy.

Some days it feels like motherhood just takes,
But my heart I have handed to you
And I'll hold yours for ever
Even when it breaks.

But right now, in this moment
You're deliciously young
Full of child's play, questions
Cuddles and fun.

No matter what, there's one constant
Each season I have you
Happy birthday, my darling
Today you turn two.

Loving Them with You

They say the trenches can bring you closer
although it takes some time
But the light is very hard to see
when there is so far out to climb.

These early years of giving
as a father, and a mother
Remembering all the many things
and forgetting about each other.

The musical beds, and little heads
that rest next to our own
Holding each other from afar
with the heartbeat of our home.

So much is left unsaid now
with no time left in the day
This love is what we know
and not so much what we say.

But every day I see you in them
in all the things you do
In all the ways you love them
and the ways you love me too.

They've broken us down and built us up
they've made us who we are
It's hard to remember it started with us
when between us feels so far.

The trenches won't last for ever
we'll look back on this time
A family we grew together
and I'll take your hand in mine.

I know some days are hard
but I'm loving them with you
I guess I'm saying I see you
and I hope you see me too.

My Favourite

People sometimes ask of my favourite days,
and I think of you being placed in my arms.
So small and new with those perfect wrinkles.
Those little cries I didn't yet recognize.
At times I needed holding too,
but oh, how I loved holding you.
Never had I felt so complete on empty.
Those slow-motion days now harder to glimpse.
You are the sun to my rise,
as I think back to my favourite days.

And then I wasn't supporting your neck any more,
you were bouncing around on my hip instead.
Suddenly you were crawling and so was I,
discovering your new view with you
and all you would get into.
You wore your personality with pride,
and as your confidence grew so did mine.
My heart was open and you filled it up.
You are the softness to my edges,
as I think back to my favourite days.

And then you were standing,
and I was standing a little taller too.
Growing into myself with you.
You were the chaos that gave me life.

As you took your first wobbly step you looked at me.
'Is this OK?' you asked with your eyes.
'It's OK,' I nodded back.
And off you went.
I'd do anything for you.
You are the piece to my puzzle,
as I think back to my favourite days.

And now you're growing into those bloated cheeks,
a little boy before my eyes.
I think of the way your hand fits in mine,
The way you say, 'I love you, Mummy.'
You are the beat to my heart.
We're lying on your bedroom floor and you're
soaring your toy car in the air.
'It's REALLY fast. Mummy, it's my favourite car.'
I look at you and tell you it's my favourite too.

My absolute favourite.

Dear Second Child

My second child,
You may have come in that order, but you aren't second-rate.
The only second you are to me is my second language.
The one I had to learn because you were so different to my first.
My second wind, when things get too much, and some days they
do, you give me the grace to be patient with myself.
My second nature, yes, you're your own little person,
but things were a little easier this time round.
I rested into it without the resistance of a first-time mum.
My second skin, I treasure our cuddles under a blanket
where I can breathe you in like an old book.
I'll admit, I wasn't up every second checking if you
were breathing in your cot; I could feel it in
my heart's rhythm while I slept.
I didn't check my app quite as often as to whether you were the
size of a lime or an avocado, and your scrapbook hasn't come
together yet . . . in fact it's still a thought in my mind.
Yes, your clothes might be second-hand and the milestone
photos aren't as planned out; sometimes they're a few days late.
You hear me yell more than I'd like to admit; you didn't arrive
into peace and quiet, my soft, sing-song voice is usually
interrupted by a crash somewhere and then more yelling.
I hear myself often saying 'Hold on a second,'
'Wait a second.' But this doesn't mean you come second.
Please don't give that a second thought.

I may not be able to give you everything you want,
but I will always try to give you everything you need;
please never second-guess that.
Know in your little core how special you are to me.
Yes, you are my second child,
not the second half of my heart but the other half.
You didn't make me a mama,
but you've made me the mama I am proud to be.
I'd move mountains for you in seconds.
And, my second child, my love for you is second to none.

Not Every Day is Beautiful

Not every day is beautiful
But you are
I can't wait for some days to end
But you're my beginning
My middle
My meeting place
Some moments I just want to be alone
Even though every moment with you is perfect
It doesn't always feel like that though
Not in that moment
When plans fall over
When no one sleeps
When I'm overwhelmed
You may deplete me some days
But you complete me every day
You're the bags under my eyes at all hours of the night
My tears of fatigue
You're also
My heart
My breath
You're the ground that brings me to my knees
The ground you walk on I adore
My grounding
You're my weakness

And the strength that I need
The build-up
The break-down
My vulnerability
You are the tune I hum
My scream
My follow
My fall
My finding
The broth of my bones
My skin
My thoughts before and after
You are mine but not mine to keep
But you keep all of me
Even though I ache
Even though some days are so very hard
Even though I doubt I'm doing this right
Not every moment is beautiful
But you are
You are the promise of love in a tired storm
Even though I may wish some moments away
You're the hands of the clock I will to stand still
And I am at the hands of you.

You are the promise of love in a tired storm

BEAUTIFUL CHAOS, JESSICA URLICHS

Just to Let You Know

Just to let you know,
I love looking at them, looking at you.
Their world.
You're still mine, you know, but I've made room.
They are at my centre and they're at yours too.
And I love you for that.

I love you for loving them more than anything.
I love how you open your arms wide to them, no matter what.
I love how they will run to you when they've
made a mistake, not away.
I love how the whole house lights up when
your car pulls in the driveway.
I love how they smell a bit like them and a bit
like you after you've given them cuddles.
I love how you let them feel, let them be them, let me be me.
I love the man you were, but more so the man you
became when you entered into fatherhood.

I don't tell you often, I know.
Life got busy, didn't it?
But I adore this life with you.
I adore us.

Just to let you know.

Not 'Just'

You are not 'just' anything
Not just a woman
Or just a friend
A wife
A partner
Or just a mother
You are a universe
Made up of waves that brought life
Stars that hold dreams
Landscapes of home
Rocks that will crumble but will always remain
The wind's gentle sway, and strongest roar
You are someone's 'all'
And 'all' is not lost
You are a mother
But never, just.

You are
a mother
But never,
just.

BEAUTIFUL CHAOS, JESSICA URLICHS

Today You Turn Three

Here we are
How the time has flown by
The fastest and slowest
Years of my life.

It's hard and it's beautiful
There's been laughter and tears
And so many lessons
In just three short years.

The battle of wills
The watching you grow
Your smile more knowing
Your brow more furrowed.

Our walks much longer
Everything still so new
And I take it all in now
Because of you.

You're my greatest teacher
More than you could know
I'd press pause if I could
But please grow, and grow.

Stepping into your personality
Growing into those cheeks
As I sit here in awe
In these front-row seats.

And you still need me close
In the dark of the night
Like the clouds hold the rain
Or the sun lights the sky.

And though our journey
Has only begun
I'm already so proud
Just to be your mum.

It's you that I see
When I look at me
Happy birthday, my darling
Today you turn three.

A Boy Will Always Need His Mum

These moments are fleeting, little man.
No matter how hard I hold on,
they'll slip through my fingers anyway.
That's life.
Sometimes I wonder if I held on long enough.

But I hope a boy will always need his mum.

One day, your arms will dangle at your sides instead
of reaching for me to pick you up.
In fact, I think that has happened already.
You won't need your sore knee kissed, or my cuddles before bed.
I'll remember the times I wished for my
nights back and realize then that I got them.

And I'll hope a boy will always need his mum.

You'll stop running into our bedroom in the morning,
sometimes before sunrise, when our tired bones ache the most.
You'll stop climbing into the sheets and demanding we get up.
Instead, I'll wake up and you'll be in the kitchen,
pouring milk into your cereal.
I'll look at you then, and realize things are much easier now,
and somehow harder too.

And I'll hope a boy will always need his mum.

You'll stop calling out for me in the middle of the night, I won't
know when the last time that I'll come running will be.
You won't tell me you love me five times a day. I hope you still
tell me, but it won't be with those little hands on my cheeks.
It just won't.
And that's OK.

And I'll hope a boy will always need his mum.

You'll let go of my hand one day, you'll tell me you can
walk the rest of the way to school on your own.
You'll give me a hug that never lasts long enough.
I don't recognize your smell quite the same,
but I still see a glimpse of those toddler cheeks,
and I'll wonder if I'll always see my baby.

And I'll hope a boy will always need his mum.

Then one day, you'll be a man holding a baby of your own.
I'll tell you he's an old soul, just like you were.
You'll smile because I'm teaching you things about
yourself you didn't know, and I'll smile because
you've been doing that to me for years.

I'll know then that you'll always need your mum,
just in different ways.
That's how I wanted to raise you.

So, I'll hold on to those precious cuddles.
I'll keep picking you up.
I'll run to you in the night as long as you call.

Because one day,
even when you need me less,
you'll know that I'll be there.

Growing Up

This year it's my hand you hold.
It's my arms you fall into.
It's my neck that catches the fall of your tears.
I'm the one you look to when you're proud of something,
or when you seek comfort.
I'm the one who can change your mood by singing a song or
knowing how to make you giggle.
I'm the keeper of your achievements and vulnerabilities.
I'm the open book that has pages waiting
to be filled with our adventures.

As we fill them up together, you'll be growing.
Year by year.
The chapter of just us will suddenly come to an end.
Before I know it, someone else's hand will take my place
and you'll be looking back at me, waving goodbye.
Your new safe place will be them,
and I'll love them too for that very reason.
I'll be proud of how you treat them,
knowing you were always shown love here.
You may leave this home with an empty room,
but with a heart that could never be so full.

All of a sudden, your big hands will steady mine instead. And when they do, I'll always remember that little hand of yours, the one that reached out for mine, and that fit so perfectly.

Fairy Mother

There once was a little fairy
Motherhood was her name
No one knew where she went
And no one knew when she came.

Things were put away at night
Appointments and lists were made
Everything ticked along it seemed
But she began to fade.

Her wings were bent and broken
Her wand was just her hands
The glitter dust were all her wishes
And many cancelled plans.

She wondered if they saw her
And did they really see
The folding, dishes and mental load
This fairy behind the scenes?

She wondered if she showed herself
The tricks kept up her sleeve
Would it still seem like magic?
And would they still believe?

It often feels invisible
The schedules that we keep
Not just the tasks throughout the day
But all their hopes and dreams.

I know you, little fairy
Because I'm one of you too
To be in the moment and ten steps ahead
Seems all we ever do.

So breathe and set your wings down
Take a moment just to feel
I know that you feel make-believe
But I promise, you are real.

They may not see this flying fairy
and all you make come true
So dance around to your favourite song
And let them just see you.

Stay Little

I want you to stay little, and I want to watch you grow.
I want to remember your song, drifting down the hallway,
even the one at night.
The song accompanied by the pitter-patter of
feet before I lift you into our bed.
And when I need a moment,
I'll still keep you near, before this moment disappears.

So stay little, will you?

But please grow, and grow.
So one day, as you tower above me,
I may rest my head on your chest instead.
I wonder what that will be like.
How that could even be possible when right now we play
ice-cream trucks and your bottom lip still drops.
Will I remember the days I stood up even when I fell short?
Will I remember how hard and beautiful they were?

Can you stay little a bit longer?

But I love watching you grow.
Yes, you can help me with the washing,
it's OK you dropped it, let's dust it off.

Yes, you are a great helper, more than you'll ever know.
I'll read that book again, and again.
I'll watch the expressions you make before
you're able to choose them.
I've never smiled in the morning so much until we met.
And you can walk with me before our path splits in two.
You can hold my hand before you let it go.

I'll always remember you this little.
But I can't wait to watch you grow.

And a Little, I Let Go

When I first met my son, I had known him a moment and loved him a lifetime. I held him to my chest for as long as I could, but he had to be taken away shortly after. The start of sharing my heart with the world, and a little, I let go.

When I moved my son from our room into his own, I smiled at the thought of having our room back, yet I ached at his cot no longer in the window, and a little, I let go.

When my husband and I went on our first child-free date, I couldn't wait to have some 'us' time again. I left a list and my brain back at home with thoughts of our son for the remainder of the evening, and a little, I let go.

When I dropped my son off at daycare for the first time I thought of all the things I could finally get done that day. I sat in the car outside for the longest time, a cave of sadness, the stories that would become his own. No longer on my hip and yet I felt heavier, and a little, I let go.

When I turned his night light off and said goodnight, I stood in his doorway expecting a small protest; it didn't come. Part of me felt relief, and the unexpected part of me felt nostalgia for all the times he asked me to stay, and a little, I let go.

And soon there will be school; at the recent open day I stood there among a sea of little summer faces in winter and my eyes started filling up. The usual warning of a mild sting didn't come, I just started crying, I was that mum.

When I look into his eyes, all oceans and daybreak, I know it's not the letting go that saddens me . . . I can't wait to watch him grow. It's all the things that don't announce their departure, it's the push and pull of it all, the sparkle he has, the one I won't always be there to help him find should he lose it.
Please don't lose it.

But we have to step back so they can step in.
We have to let pieces of ourselves go with it.

As mothers we're faced with this daily task, and we're strong enough to see it through, we are.
But we were never designed to master it.

But we have to
step back so
they can step in.
We have to let
pieces of ourselves
go with it.

BEAUTIFUL CHAOS, JESSICA URLICHS

Today You Turn Four

I still can't believe
That you are mine
It's been four years
In my heart, a lifetime.

For though our journey
Has so far to go
Here's a few things
I want you to know.

Keep on discovering
So much is still new
Keep dreaming and loving
Please keep on being you.

Keep asking questions
With that curious face
You always belong
Know that I'm your safe place.

Keep on believing
You can reach the sky
Keep smiling, keep laughing
Know it's OK to cry.

Keep being brave
Know you're never alone
When the clouds hide the sun
There's a light on at home.

Keep weaving your kindness
Around others like string
Never lose that sparkle
That makes your soul sing.

And as we keep growing
As I watch you shine
I'll realize that you
Were never truly mine.

Just a flower I watched
Begin to unfurl
The greatest privilege
To share my heart with the world.

I'll always look at you
With immeasurable awe
Happy birthday, my darling
Today you turn four.

I Do Not Know Everything

And so you see,
I do not know everything.
Where those birds are flying to or
the dog's name outside the supermarket.
I don't know if Superman is stronger than the other
superhero in your hand, or where his head has gone.
I don't know if I can forget the time you said,
'Don't explode' – I still think about that.
I don't know where these days have gone, or how much longer
your head will rest on this pillow shoulder.

I don't know if I am more mother or woman
and in all my urgency –
will you stand tall next to me, in the blink of an eye
(right now we touch noses when I pull on your sweater).

For I am no fortune-teller, no philosopher or great leader.
I am but your mother,
Who could trace your face in the low light of the morning.
Who feels your eyes light up, like I am a sunseeker.
Who knows the moulds of each cuddle, from each age.
And I have stayed awake,
I have stayed awake.

And I know your laugh and your cry because it lives inside me,
and how to hold your heart
while the stars burn in the sky.

And so you see, I do not know everything,
But I know you're my why.
For now.
For always.
For ever.

You're my why.
For now.
For always.
For ever.

BEAUTIFUL CHAOS, JESSICA URLICHS

Just a Minute

He asks me to watch how fast he can run,
how high he can jump, 'Did you see that, Mum?'
'Just a minute,' I say –
'I'm almost done.'

He asks me to listen while he hums a tune,
'Just a second,' I say –
'I'll be there soon.'

He asks me to play, as I turn away,
I have things to do, and don't have all day.
'Hold on a moment,' he hears me say.

He asks me to look at a picture he drew,
I say I will soon, but I've things to do.

For his world is in colour, a work of art.
An invite he offers into his heart.
But there's something unfinished.
Always something to start.

I will never be done
There will always be more
The dust will still settle
on some endless chore.

And the running, the jumping,
the 'Mummy, watch this.'
Will I remember it only as something I missed?
Too busy with crossing things off my list?

Let's sit for a while, let's take some time.
Pull me into your world,
Let me step out of mine.

He soars around, his arms are wings,
And I finally learn that we need the same things,
In this season, and all that it brings.

A boy and his mother,
Just seeing each other.

Pull me into
your world,
Let me step
out of mine.

BEAUTIFUL CHAOS, JESSICA URLICHS

Mothering in the Darkness

I cried yesterday, not just because I didn't sleep, but because I heard the kids at the table laughing, pancakes being made, our Sunday ritual, as I lay in the room with the curtains drawn.

Then suddenly it's 1 a.m., I can hear the waves of white noise, I can hear a suck swallow, my husband snoring, even the cat's snoring, suck swallow, and some more snoring. My eyes are barely open. My toes are now unclenched and I'm looking down at how beautiful she is, still amazed that only days ago she wasn't in my arms.

There's just something so tender about mothering in the darkness, when your breasts are sore, your bedside table is full, and you're healing and breaking all at once. Even when the mother in you has lived these nights before, she's still new and emerging in different ways, with each new babe.

I can hear a faint cry out down the hallway, which means my husband gets to sleep properly in one of the kid's beds now, what once seemed like a chore.

There's more snuffling coming from the bassinet, as a layer of sleep is being ripped away. The familiar thought of 'How will I do this?' sets in, but these are the days of postpartum.

Raw, brutal, magical, honest.
And I will do this, as I've done before, like all mothers do.

I lift up her perfect tiny frame and bring her in close,
as the night turns to day,
by day,
by day.

Dear Husband (the future can wait)

Dear Husband,

There's a life in the future with little faces in photo frames instead of before our eyes. Artwork and ABC magnets won't adorn our fridge, and these old leggings I'm wearing right now will be long gone.

There's a bed big enough, where little elbows and knees won't prod us in our sleep, and only our feet will swing out in the morning.

There's a vase placed in reach of little arms because there aren't any, and mugs will daringly sit on the edge of the table.

There's a bank balance that looks a bit more forgiving, a bag I leave with that isn't overflowing, and it will only take us ten seconds from the door to the car.

There's a free calendar that isn't packed with swimming lessons, dance classes and muddy sports shoes. And we'll get to know each other for a third time, before them, with them, and then when only two jackets hang at the door.

There's a clean car, the only noise is the hum of the radio. There will be no endless questions in a high-pitched voice from the back seat, there may even be days we don't hear from them at all.

There's a date night with no curfew, my mum's not
needed for babysitting, and we aren't sleeping with one
eye open, waiting for the shuffle of feet down the hallway.
A type of freedom that feels heavy.

There's a house that's clean, maybe our couch is new, and we
aren't stepping on Lego or toy cars either. In fact, there's not
much colour anywhere; remember how we hated all the colour?
Remember how it came with so much happiness?

There's a dinner table that feels big, we aren't negotiating bites
of vegetables, or wiping little hands and mouths. But sometimes
there's a knock on the door and the table is full once more.

There's a shower that doesn't sound like baby cries, a coffee that
is warm, and my body will be my own. We won't wear tired the
same way, but time will have aged us anyway.

There will be hard moments to come that will make these
moments look easy, but we'll remember.
We'll remember the first words, the curls, the 'I love you's, the
moments we almost broke, and how we held each other through
it. We'll laugh and we'll cry, just like we did then.

There's a life in the future and it's coming for us every day.
So let's get swept up in the beautiful chaos in front of us.
Let's make the future wait a little longer.
Because I love this life with you so much,
this one right now.

*Let's get swept
up in the
beautiful chaos
in front of us.
Let's make the
future wait a
little longer.*

BEAUTIFUL CHAOS, JESSICA URLICHS

Stay-at-home Mum

The house is a mess
My clothes are old
The chores are endless
As the day unfolds.

Guilt is a feeling
I've grown to know
It follows me daily
Like a dismal shadow.

Aches and pains
And all the strains
Bending and lifting
And playing games.

Stay-at-home mum
Won't that be fun
Finger-painting and Netflix
And one on one.

'No more work for you,' they'd say.
'Free to relax and play all day.'

'Naive' is a word
Not a strong enough fit
To describe this exhaustion
That fills every bit.

My back is sore
My hands are dry
My lunch will be crusts
My outlet a cry.

I'm working on forgiveness
I'm working on myself
I'm trying to locate her
High up on a shelf.

I'm in the best company
But still, I feel lonely
These windows grew bars
For somewhere so homely.

I'm juggling many balls
But that's not the worst
One's about to drop
Which one will fall first?

I hate asking for help
Don't you see, I can do this
But I need it some days
When it all feels so useless.

Resentment and woes
The highs and the lows
Unconditional love
And that's how it goes.

Feelings drifting
So hard to pin down
Some days you win
Others you drown.

Yes, I am lucky
I love them to bits
And I'd do it again
Every day for these kids.

They've helped me slow down
They've taught me to say 'No'
They're teaching me daily
About how I can grow.

I'm better because of them
I'll continue to be
A love like no other
As they are for me.

We're stay-at-home mums
We're bloody strong
So we keep on
Keeping on.

Rubbish Day

These days a bed with us both
doesn't need a baby between
for us to be separate
or feel unseen

a thought of you is quickly replaced
about them, or the chores
or shrugging off your embrace

never far from apart
as you pull me in close
a beautiful battle
of who needs me the most

my energy drained bit by bit
my arms pulled to elastic
my hair fraying like a ragdoll
what to do with your compliments
when my reflection's so fragile

it's not your fault
you see me the same
mum, mummy, babe, honey
I've forgotten my name

my heart is so full yet it's still healing
I open my mouth and speak
words with no feeling

we talk when it's dark and all is done
once the trials from the day
are razor sharp on my tongue

and to extend further warmth
just feels like a chore
there's no pictures of just us
on my phone any more

it's not that I don't love you, I do
more than ever
it's the ships we've become
drifting off in the weather

and I long to fall into those arms
so much
but I don't quite know what to do
with your touch

I know beautiful and ragged
become one and the same
when we speak of mothers
when we speak of this change

it shouldn't be such an effort, should it?
to be a mother, a wife, a lover
and everything I was before and after

I love how you try
with all of your strength
to break down my walls
while I hold you at length

it's all I imagined
bum pats over dishes
while our babes are tucked up
it's not perfect, yet it is

I watched you with the kids the other night
it felt warm in my chest
everything felt right

I smiled
tell him
TELL HIM
you looked up
and I swallowed
'are you taking out the bins?'

My After All

I'm beginning to think
You may be the last
I want it to slow
But it's going so fast.

Never say never
But I think it is true
The last babble and crawl
Will be with you.

These 'last's feel quite different
As I loosen my grip
On the milestones we pass
On this one-way trip.

See, as hard as it is
Some days where I sink
I could do it again
But we won't I don't think.

How can you be done
With a love at the start
That has no end
That opens your heart?

The last time you happily
Sat on my hip
Fell asleep in my arms
Wore your last bib.

See, some of these lasts
I can't quite pin down
You won't lie here with me
The way you do now.

Though it was yesterday
It'll feel like a while
Since I heard a first word
Or saw a first smile.

No you weren't my first
But I was your first love
And for you I've slowed down
For you, I've become.

My heart was full
But you made it expand
I grew the most
When you took my hand.

I guess I'm worried
That I won't remember
But who could forget
The final love letter?

Yes, there's goodbyes
Times unforgiving
But I know in my heart
This is just the beginning.

I'll hold you longer
So I can recall
You are not the last
But my after all.

And for you I've
slowed down
For you,
I've become.

BEAUTIFUL CHAOS, JESSICA URLICHS

Will You Remember?

Will you remember
to way back before
I whispered 'I love you'
as I closed your door?

And sometimes I wonder
if you will remember
the way the house smelt
in the month of December.

The racing to bed
and stroking your head
the songs that we sang
and the books that we read.

I wonder if maybe
you'll remember on Sunday
the pancakes, then school bags
all ready for Monday.

That mother spelt love
and the way I held you
that when I messed up
I apologized too.

I wonder if maybe
you'll remember the way
his keys made music
at the end of the day.

How I held you for ever
when our eyes first met
how you'll never remember
what I can't forget.

One day you'll be older
maybe a child of your own
and I'll sit there and watch you
and that's when I'll know.

It was more than just holding you in my arms
And more than just conversations with the stars.
It was more than the nights that called for my bed,
the ones I stayed up and held you instead.
It was more than the milestones, or the places we'd been.
It was the little moments too, the ones in between.
And some days were hard, sometimes a lot.
And we muddled through often.
More often than not.
But the love and the smiles would find us each morning.
The glue to our days of this childhood forming.

And maybe one night
after the longest of days
when you're singing about
happiness when skies are grey.

There were Sunday pancakes
and it's now time for bed
as you yawn at the stars
while you're stroking their head.

Maybe you'll ask me,
'Will they remember this, Mum?'
your face will be tired
your hair in a bun.

And that's when I'll smile
because now I am sure
as you whisper, 'I love you,'
and close their door.

My Resumé

Sorry I'm late,
I should have updated my CV!
What have I been doing
So far on this degree?

Well, I've done some nursing
I've done some juggling too
I'm also good at herding cats
With feeding time at the zoo
And I'm quite the illusionist
With peek-a-boo.

I'm a great nursery-rhyme singer
Thinking of joining a choir
And sometimes at night
I'm a human pacifier.

But don't put that last part down
Because that would be weird.

I'm a researcher and an analyst
I work through many problems
I can handle all sorts of challenges
Throw them at me, I'll solve them.

I'm an experienced hygienist
Nightly baths are my profession
Oh no, I'm not talking about myself
Sorry, what was your question?

I've had some workplace injuries
Someone called it a 'rod for my back'
But somehow I survived
With endurance and not giving a crap.

I'm also an event planner
I'm a taxi and a chef
A stylist and a storyteller
And a great cleaner of mess.

I'm a director and a producer
And let me just recap
References during lunch is out
My boss will be taking a nap.

I'm a teacher and a student
Sometimes that line is blurred
I'm a mediator and a builder
And I translate words
What language, you ask?
Oh, you wouldn't have heard.

I'm a heavyweight champion
A bodyguard, a judge
A chemist and a life coach
And I don't hold a grudge.

What do I do in my spare time?
I go for walks around the street
Looking like utter ass
Muttering, 'Please go to sleep.'

What are my key attributes?
Well, I'm braver now and stronger
I'm confident in my choices
I can push myself a little longer.

I'm a multitasker, a sleep consultant
And by that, I mean a hammock
I love taking photos of my family
That look more like *National Geographic*.

I'm a financial planner, a shift worker
An impressionist, an assistant
An inspector and a detector
No day is ever consistent.

I'm also quite the tour guide
And pretty good, I'm told
I know I only have two arms
But you should see how much I can hold.

My weakness is, I guess
I feel everything 10 x more
Since becoming someone's home
I'm somewhat different than before.

My last salary for all this work?
No, I didn't charge a fee
It's the greatest 'job' I ever had
I'd do it all again for free.

Today You Turn Five

I watch you and I wonder
When you got so tall
How you can seem so big
When you're still so very small.

A backpack and a uniform
Will hang upon your frame
I love to watch you grow
But can things just stay the same?

Just for a moment more
Just for a little while
Before the toddler completely vanishes
From those cheeks and from that smile.

Those fingerprints are fading
From the windows where they climbed
And things are ever-changing
A constant promise that is time.

Can we still share little stories?
When more and more become your own?
When I ask you what you did today
Will you tell me when we get home?

Suddenly my days aren't filled
With quite as much of you
Yet in my heart, and in my mind
That couldn't be less true.

And though the seasons change
You'll be my baby for ever
When did you get so wise?
When did you get so clever?

But for now, your big expressions
Still catch you by surprise
And every time I see your face
It's like we first locked eyes.

You've turned my world to magic
You've made colours come alive
Happy birthday to you, my darling
Today you turn five.

Here's to Us

Here's to us.

I remember us, young, carefree us.
Plans were only made for travel, and 'routine' was as
good as the empty pages of our calendar.

Sheets would lie lazily around us on Sunday mornings
and new café ventures would await.
Now the sheets are cold at 4 a.m.
but the floor next to the cot is warm.

The touch of each other's hands has been replaced by soft,
beautifully grubby little ones.
Our excitement used to lie in the discoveries about each other,
now they're with each little new word or babble, each new curl.

We sigh a lot, usually as a response to a question,
'How was your day?' Sigh.
When I throw my arms around you it's to lean on you,
and you know that, and that's OK.

We brush past each other like drifting
clouds through the night-time routine.

We forget to say I love you out loud sometimes,
but we have a language that we've developed in support instead;
the 'I love you's are still there.

Our days were mapped by arbitrary decisions, currently they're
dictated by leaps, phases and regressions; I know we didn't want
to be 'those parents', but here we are.

We're completely and vulnerably honest with each other,
not just in words, but in our deepest emotions and letting them
float to the surface.

We've seen a lot, you've seen a lot of me.
At my worst, I've said things I'm not proud of in
the heat of the moment, and I'm sorry.

I want to thank you though, for everything.
For seeing through the unfamiliarity and knowing
I'm still there, but loving the new me even more,
and loving what we've created more than life itself.

We discover so much when we first become parents and
we forget that our relationship is a new discovery too.

Us has a new meaning now, it's us and them.

Encompassing and evolving and I love you
for supporting and loving me through it all.

Here's to us.

Us has a new meaning now, it's us and them.

BEAUTIFUL CHAOS, JESSICA URLICHS

Looking for Her

I've been looking for her a little bit lately, the old me.

I've been missing her, my husband, balance.
The scales have been tipping for a long time.

I've either been out of my mind or inside it too much.

It still feels like we're in the thick of it,
even though there's no newborn any more.

Chat is usually about things like having showers at
night to save time in the morning, kisses are rushed or missed,
'goodbye's are muffled through closed doors.

I'm then gathering up the things to leave the house with.
I find myself sitting in the car with the kids in a dishevelled state,
unsure where we're going. I wonder how I look to others now,
do I LOOK like a mum?

I'm still confused, I know I need to eat better but if
I'm ever alone in the car I find myself scoffing
McDonald's at the lights like an animal.

I'm confused how some days I can feel like a lioness,
and others a chameleon, still trying to 'fit in'.

I'm confused why people tell me to enjoy every moment. I'm
certain I'm growing more through the ones I've enjoyed the least.

I'm confused by when I talk about how hard self-discovery can
be through motherhood, I always feel the need to tie
it up with a 'but I wouldn't trade it for anything'.
Of course I wouldn't. I don't need to validate it, just leave it
untied as the endless string of moments it's meant to be.

I'm confused.
What do I even enjoy any more?

This 'Me' in 'Mum', this motherhood-lined jacket that
some days doesn't warm up and others fits just right.

I wonder if motherhood truly does strip you back,
or is it just another layer entirely, so consuming that
breaking it down to our core simply takes time?

What I do know though is it isn't necessarily about going
back to the 'old you', old jeans, old lifestyle, old body.

It's about becoming.

Maybe I have to stop looking for 'Her',
so that she can come and find me.

May He Always Know

Dear little boy,
you have not journeyed far
but these things I will tell you,
you already are.

Just some small reminders
to follow your dreams,
to continue being strong,
and what strength truly means.

Strength doesn't always
come from the loudest,
the one who talks most,
the one who's the proudest.

Strength can be quiet,
pride knows how to listen,
creates beauty from shadows
and not just things that glisten.

Strength can be dancing,
or running a mile,
lending a hand,
or sharing a smile.

It's also about giving,
for some will just take.
You have courage, little one,
let it mend things that break.

Strength is in showing
how to lead from your heart,
and sometimes, my boy,
it will set you apart.

Your friends should uplift you,
you always have a choice,
to stay, or walk away,
let your heart be your voice.

Strength can be your body,
strength can be your mind,
you can lift heavy things,
and be gentle and kind.

Strength is in loving,
it is letting yourself feel,
tears are strength too,
they allow us to heal.

Let the sun touch your face,
let art run through your veins.
It's OK to be fearful.
It's OK to feel pain.

You are brave, you are bold,
may you shine, may you grow,
with the strongest of hearts,
may you always know.

Strength can be many things,
though you've not journeyed far,
I will always love you,
for exactly who you are.

May She Always Know

I want my daughter
to know her own strength,
to know love without borders,
and dream at great length.

I hope she is brave,
and I hope she reads books,
when people say she's pretty –
she'll know it's more than her looks.

For she's pretty smart,
and she's pretty kind.
May she be heard for her voice,
and seen for her mind.

As she grows into a woman
I hope she stands strong,
for some will try to knock her,
but I hope she holds on.

Because her power is great,
and cannot be measured,
her passion and vulnerability
should always be treasured.

May she know the difference
between right and wrong,
not because of some rules,
but what is in her heart's song.

May she question the narrative,
make choices, speak clear,
may she never repeat herself
out of doubt or fear.

May she strive for big things
in a world that screams thin,
just as a man's size does not define him.

I hope she sticks up for those who need it,
herself included; I hope she believes it.

May no one dim her light,
May it shine,
May it grow.
What a force that she is.
May she always know.

*May she know
the difference
between right
and wrong,
not because of
some rules,
but what is in
her heart's song.*

BEAUTIFUL CHAOS, JESSICA URLICHS

With You

Oh, how there are a million things to do
And I'll do them, I will
I'll do those too
But right now
I'll just be,
Here,
With you.

Oh, how I want to sleep, I do
And one day, I will
I'll sleep right through
But right now
I'll just be,
Here,
With you.

Oh, how the days are long, it's true
Yesterdays are many
But todays are few
So I'll fill them up
With all of you
And simply be,
Here,
With you.

Meant to be

The nights would become a burden that would breathe
down my neck during the days.

And sometimes I would cry, to myself, to my husband.

She was the reason for my tears, and I was the answer to hers.

It's not that I don't remember it,
but the sharp inhale of it all has faded.

Last night, she called out for me, and I went to her,
like I always have.
The hallways aren't tunnels like they used to be.

She whispered to me that I was her best friend
in that little lisp of hers and kissed my nose.
She pulled my face in so we were breathing one and the same.
I could feel her lashes on my cheek.
She traced the wrinkles around my eyes, the ones I'm newly
self-conscious about.
The ones she couldn't care less about.
And wrapped her arms around me,
knowing it would be harder for me to sneak away.
And I let her.

Because I don't want to forget the way she looks at me
as if I scattered the stars in the sky.

I close my eyes instead of waiting for her arm to soften.
No longer feeling like an island.
No longer up and down all night.
Just there as she drifts off, until it will be no longer.

We never 'cracked the code' of sleep.
But as I lie here now,
I think it was meant to be this way,
for both of us.

For You, I Would Do Anything

I won't always be your everything
But for you, I would do anything.

I'll climb the highest mountain
If you are on the other side
But for now I'll lay here with you
For another sleepless night.

I'll be your music maker
Right from the very start
The one who sings your language
Who knows you off by heart.

I'll be your open book
We will write in it together
With pages left unnumbered
So our story lasts for ever.

For you I can be magic
Though your spell on me is best
How you can be right there
And the drumbeat in my chest.

I'll always be your strength
When I'm tired, more than ever
I'll stare at you for hours
Like my eyes are finding treasure.

I'll be your address
Even when you're old and grown
I'll hold on to your worries
As if they were my own.

For you I'd walk through fire
A pain I won't forget
I've done it once before
The moment that we met.

I promise I'll stop rushing
For you I'll change my pace
Nothing will be perfect
But your ever-changing face.

I'll be the one who loves you
As far as the eye can see
I'll try and teach you what I know
But it's you that will teach me.

For you I'll be the stars
For you I'll be the moon
But mostly I'll be me
Like I was handpicked for you.

I won't always get it right
I won't always be your everything
But I'll always be your mum
And for you, I would do anything.

*For you I'll
be the stars
For you I'll
be the moon
But mostly
I'll be me
Like I was
handpicked
for you.*

BEAUTIFUL CHAOS, JESSICA URLICHS

If You were a Love Note

If time were made of colour
you'd be my golden hour.
If love was just a seed
you'd be each and every flower.
If the sky could whisper secrets
you'd be its wind and summer rain.
If the morning sun had arms
you'd be held again, again, again.
If my heartbeat was a language
you'd be its love letter at dawn.
If stardust formed a trail on earth
It would take me to when you were born.

If time were made of colour you'd be my golden hour.

BEAUTIFUL CHAOS, JESSICA URLICHS

The Unseen

I'm proud of you for rising before light,
buttering toast in the dark, after another long night.
I'm proud of you, even when you're cracked open you
shine in a way that shows you're not broken.
I'm proud of you and the way that you mother,
the strength that it takes, being that place for another.
I'm proud of you as you move to those cries,
knowing sunrise is honest, but sunset lies.
I'm proud of you, and the weight in your arms,
a small head that won't rest, unless in your palms.
I'm proud of you, as you shift through the day,
with hope, and then tears, that their littleness won't stay.
These days are small castles you are building from dreams.
I'm proud of the work you're doing in the unseen.

*These days
are small castles
you are building
from dreams.*

BEAUTIFUL CHAOS, JESSICA URLICHS

The Ways I Will Know You

I tell myself I'll remember all of you,
but this I cannot promise you.
Even now, memories are fading,
the way your voice sounded two years ago,
the way when I close my eyes I try to replay
you like a live photo that dances under my thumb.
But it doesn't, not quite.

It's unfair really, we grapple so hard to hold on to
the moments of these early years, the years of first smiles,
white noise and first words.
The years we so desperately try to be present in,
but never truly know how.
The hard years, offered in fragments. The years filtered in
fatigue, one big, beautiful blur.
It's unfair how we never really stood a chance.
Because no matter how hard I stare at you, your profile changes
before my eyes, leaving behind an outline of what once was.
The way the waves leave wisps that draw ever-changing patterns
across the sand. I was here, they say. Just moments ago.

But this I have come to accept.
There will be moments that will fade like photographs,
and with them, some of the details. But not all.

I remember your smell every time I breathed you in for a kiss.
I remember how your voice was a roller coaster of highs and
lows when telling me stories, especially the ones before bed.
I remember the warm brown of your eyes as a toddler,
how they haven't changed, how it's such a comfort
that they haven't changed.
I remember how expressions would stun you, surprise you.
I remember the first time you saw a dead monarch
butterfly; you were so little that you didn't know about death,
you decided it was sick, you decided it needed its mummy.

It hurts, because though there is only one of you, there have
been so many of you in my life already. I can't promise you
I won't forget, because some things, I will.
I saw it all, I saw all of you, but my memory will forever be at
the mercy of its choosing.

But this growing of us together lives in my bones,
what we've learnt runs through my veins,
and the versions of you live in my heart.

I may not be able to close my eyes and see every detail.
But I will know them.

Like how eyes know to cry.
Like how lips know to smile.
Like how leaves fall, and they don't remember.
They just know.
They just do.

Though there is only one of you, there have been so many of you in my life already.

BEAUTIFUL CHAOS, JESSICA URLICHS

I Love You, and I Miss Me

I love you, and sometimes I miss me.

I miss thoughts that aren't broken. Conversations that aren't
always interrupted. I miss being able to finish a sentence without
stopping midway to scramble for a word I use every day.

I love you, and I miss spontaneity, the way I used to dream
ridiculous things with the notion they might actually happen
that very next day. I miss throwing caution to the wind and
not being so accountable all the time.

I love you, and I miss sleep, I am worn thin, in love, and in this
labour of love. It's the hardest thing I will ever do, yet it's never
been easier loving you. But my eyes are open so often through
the night that I wake up feeling broken, digging my heels into
what feels like glass for another day.

I love you, and I miss slow Sundays; the turbulence of
our days sometimes has me barely recognizing myself
in the mirror. The way I don't recognize my voice sometimes,
the way I know I shouldn't have yelled, the way
your forgiveness somehow hurts more.

I love you, and I miss not worrying so much. The world used to scare me, and now it petrifies me, because I can't shelter you in these arms for ever, I can't protect you from pain. You'll feel it all and so will I, your happiness will make my heart shift and your sadness will lodge itself there too.

I love you, and I miss not sharing my food, my body, my bed. And yet these are all the things I love more than ever, but I miss alone time also, and I miss eating a meal that isn't rushed, so I can taste it, talk with my husband before 9 p.m. about things other than our to-do list.

I miss these things sometimes.
And yet, these things pale in comparison to watching you smile when you achieve something, the way your eyes flutter closed as I'm stroking your forehead, the way I watch you be brave, or caring, or curious. The way – in some ways – I feel more 'me' than ever with you. It's the busiest I've ever been, and yet it's gradual and gentle. I love you.
I would choose you every time; I'm just finding little ways to choose me too right now, so I can be better.
For me.
For you.

When I Leave This Place

If I wasn't here, my love,
If I suddenly was to leave
Without notice, a kiss, some parting words,
You mean everything to me.

It's hard to imagine with you right now,
The beating of my heart,
My soul, my centre, my little shadow,
That we could ever be apart.

And when I think of my life before
A time that I met you
I wonder if leaving will feel the same.
Will I again become someone new?

My proudest moment was meeting you,
My heart song is your laughter,
I hardly remember life before
And you'll mostly remember after.

My bones and my body know you
From the moment you started to grow.
Will the way that I loved you be enough
If I suddenly was to go?

You'll see me in the flowers,
You'll hear me in the breeze,
I'll live on in your heart,
Close your eyes and you'll see me.

I'll cuddle you in your shadows
If you need me, and you might.
I'll be the sunshine on your face
In the morning's dappled light.

For I only have but two great fears,
One's a world without you in it,
My second is leaving you far too soon
As my love for you is infinite.

I guess I'll never truly know
When that one day might be
But in case for ever doesn't come
You mean everything to me.

Acknowledgements

Thank you to my editors at Penguin, especially Emily Robertson, who reached out to me. Your encouragement and support in my words means more than you know. Thank you to Gemma Douglas, the first person to re-post my work, who gave me the courage to keep being vulnerable. Thank you to my friends, who have championed me along the way, the ones I've had for years, (Courtenay Street, I am talking about you), and the new ones I have made online. Thank you to my readers: those little messages of encouragement, the ones you thought wouldn't mean much, have meant the most. Thank you to my mother, the strongest lady I know. Thank you to my husband, for most incredible support, and for listening to me read my finished pieces (even when you've been falling asleep), and to my children. My inspiration, my love, my soul.

Author Photo © David Muir Photo - Wedding Photographer

JESSICA URLICHS is a *Sunday Times* bestselling author and poet who lives in New Zealand with her husband and three children. She has written a variety of children's books to help babies and young children navigate their emotions in their early years. Jess's honest and heartfelt poetry about her family and motherhood continue to be a source of guidance for mothers and parents alike around the world to connect.

AUTHOR ONLINE PRESENCE

JessicaUrlichs.com

JessUrlichs

JessUrlichs

JessicaUrlichs